A Visual Dictionary of a
COLONIAL COMMUNITY

Bobbie Kalman

🌱 **Crabtree Publishing Company**

www.crabtreebooks.com

Crabtree Visual Dictionaries
Created by Bobbie Kalman

Für meine Tante Burgi,
mit vieler Liebe und wundervollen Erinnerungen

Author and Editor-in-Chief
Bobbie Kalman

Editor
Robin Johnson

Research
Candice Campbell

Illustration research
Crystal Sikkens

Design
Bobbie Kalman
Katherine Kantor

Production coordinator
Katherine Kantor

Illustrations
All illustrations by Barbara Bedell except:
Halina Below-Spada: page 21 (top left)
Katherine Kantor: page 7 (chicken)
Antoinette "Cookie" Bortolon: pages 1 (tongs), 17 (top), 18 (top),
    21 (iron toaster), 25 (pudding), 26 (top left), 27 (middle left and
    bottom right), 28 (boots), 29 (wigs), 31 (wig and shoe)
Bonna Rouse: pages 1 (all except hammer, ax, chisel, and tongs),
    4 (wheelwright), 10 (woodsman), 11 (lathe workers, cabinetmaker,
    and drawknife), 16 (top), 31 (cabinet)
Margaret Amy Salter: back cover (flowers and tea cup), border,
    pages 3 (boy and girl and purse), 4 (slave and wealthy colonists),
    24 (purse)
Tiffany Wybouw: pages 7 (carrot), 22 (top left), 29 (walking stick)

Photographs
Lewis Parker: page 16 (bottom)
© Shutterstock.com: pages 6, 16
Other images by Object Gear

Library and Archives Canada Cataloguing in Publication

Kalman, Bobbie, 1947-
    A visual dictionary of a colonial community / Bobbie Kalman.

(Crabtree visual dictionaries)
Includes index.
ISBN 978-0-7787-3502-1 (bound).--ISBN 978-0-7787-3522-9 (pbk.)

    1. United States--Social life and customs--To 1775--Dictionaries,
Juvenile. 2. United States--History--Colonial period, ca.
1600-1775--Dictionaries, Juvenile. 3. United States--Social life and
customs--To 1775--Pictorial works--Juvenile literature. 4. United
States--History--Colonial period, ca. 1600-1775--Pictorial works--Juvenile
literature. 5. Picture dictionaries--Juvenile literature. I. Title. II. Series.

E162.K195 2007   j973.203   C2007-904774-2

Library of Congress Cataloging-in-Publication Data

Kalman, Bobbie.
    A Visual dictionary of a colonial community / Bobbie Kalman.
        p. cm. -- (Crabtree visual dictionaries)
    Includes index.
    ISBN-13: 978-0-7787-3502-1 (rlb)
    ISBN-10: 0-7787-3502-8 (rlb)
    ISBN-13: 978-0-7787-3522-9 (pb)
    ISBN-10: 0-7787-3522-2 (pb)
    1. United States--Social life and customs--To 1775--Dictionaries, Juvenile. 2. United
States--History--Colonial period, ca. 1600-1775--Dictionaries, Juvenile. 3. United
States--Social life and customs--To 1775--Pictorial works--Juvenile literature. 4. United
States--History--Colonial period, ca. 1600-1775--Pictorial works--Juvenile literature. 5.
Picture dictionaries--Juvenile literature. I. Title. II. Series.

E162.K1996 2007
970.01--dc22
                                                    2007030672

Crabtree Publishing Company
www.crabtreebooks.com   1-800-387-7650
Copyright © **2008 CRABTREE PUBLISHING COMPANY**. All rights reserved. No part of this publication may be reproduced, stored in a retrieval system or be
transmitted in any form or by any means, electronic, mechanical, photocopying, recording, or otherwise, without the prior written permission of Crabtree Publishing Company. In
Canada: We acknowledge the financial support of the Government of Canada through the Book Publishing Industry Development Program (BPIDP) for our publishing activities.

Published in Canada
Crabtree Publishing
616 Welland Ave.
St. Catharines, Ontario
L2M 5V6

Published in the United States
Crabtree Publishing
PMB16A
350 Fifth Ave., Suite 3308
New York, NY 10118

Published in the United Kingdom
Crabtree Publishing
White Cross Mills
High Town, Lancaster
LA1 4XS

Published in Australia
Crabtree Publishing
386 Mt. Alexander Rd.
Ascot Vale (Melbourne)
VIC 3032

Contents

Colonial people

A **colony** is a place that is ruled by a king or other leader in another country. The colonies in North America were ruled by a king in England. People who lived in the colonies were called **colonists**. Some colonists owned big farms called **plantations**. Many plantation owners were very wealthy. Other colonists lived in towns and worked at different jobs. These pictures show how some colonists lived and the jobs they had.

Slaves were brought from Africa to work for wealthy colonists. They worked long hours in the fields and in homes. This slave is working on a tobacco plantation.

*Some colonists worked as **tradespeople**. They made things that other people needed. This **wheelwright** is making a wheel.*

reamer

iron

wagon wheel

Some wealthy colonists lived on huge plantations. Slaves cooked their meals and cleaned their homes.

*Many colonial women worked hard cooking, cleaning, washing, and ironing for their families or as **servants**.*

Blacksmiths *made things from iron.*

Many children learned job skills by working as **apprentices** *for tradespeople such as blacksmiths.*

Apothecaries *made and sold medicines. They worked in shops that were also called apotharies.*

Musicians *entertained people in* **taverns.**

Each day, the **town crier** *rang a bell and shouted out the news in town.*

There was no electricity in colonial times. People used candles to light their homes. This woman is a **chandler.** *Chandlers made candles to sell to others.*

5

Colonial homes

Colonists lived in many kinds of homes. Homes built on farms were usually small. Most homes built in towns were quite large. Many of the larger homes had **dependencies**. Dependencies were small buildings behind the homes. Animals and food were kept in these small buildings. Some dependencies are shown on the opposite page.

chimneys

*Many colonial homes had **symmetrical** designs. Symmetrical homes looked the same on both sides of their centers.*

palace

The fanciest colonial home was the Governor's Palace in Williamsburg, where the Governor of Virginia lived.

extra rooms

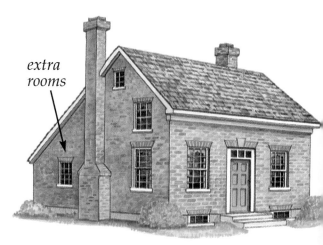

*To make their homes larger, some people added extra rooms onto the backs of their homes. This style of home is called a **saltbox**.*

People did not have running water inside their homes. They got their water from wells. This well is inside a **well house**.

Cheeses and butter were made in the **dairy**. Dairies were often built in shaded areas. Stone floors kept these buildings cool inside.

A **smokehouse** was built over a fire pit. Meat was **smoked** over the fire to keep it from going bad.

apples

butter

ham

chicken

A **cellar** was an underground room that was used to store fruits and vegetables.

Chickens lived in **coops**. Most coops had windows to let in sunlight. Many farmers believed hens laid more eggs when they had plenty of light.

7

Life on a plantation

Some colonists lived on plantations. A plantation grew mainly one type of **crop**. Crops are plants grown for human use. There were tobacco plantations, sugar plantations, and cotton plantations. The work on many plantations was done by slaves. Slaves were treated badly. They were not paid for their work and had very few rights.

1. The plantation owner and his family lived in the **Big House**.
2. The **kitchen house** was a separate building used to prepare meals.
3. Slaves spun wool into yarn in the **spinning house**.
4. Yarn was woven into cloth in the **weaving house**.
5. Clothes were made in the **sewing house**.
6. Slaves lived in the **slave quarters**. The slave quarters were near the fields.
7. **Tallow**, or fat, was melted in the **soap kettle**. Candles and soap were made in the house behind it.
8. Color was added to cloth in the **dye house**.
9. The blacksmith made tools and horseshoes in the **smithy**.
10. Furniture and coffins were made in the **carpentry shop**.
11. Sheep, cows, and other animals lived in the barn. Horses lived in the **stables**.
12. Clothes and bed sheets were washed in the **laundry**.
13. Fresh meat and milk were kept cold in the **ice house**.
14. The colonists got their water from a well or a springhouse.
15. Meat and fish were hung up and smoked over a fire in the smokehouse.
16. Carriages were kept in the **carriage house**.
17. The **bootmaker's shop** was where boots and shoes were made from leather.

tobacco plant

Many plantations grew tobacco.

scarecrow

vegetable garden

Colonial woodworkers

In colonial days, forests grew all over North America. There was plenty of wood for building homes and for making furniture and many other useful things. Tradespeople called **woodworkers** earned their living from building or carving things from wood. These pictures show some woodworkers and the things they made. Which woodworkers made barrels? Which woodworkers made furniture?

Housewrights built houses. It took several housewrights to build a house.

chimney

house frame

peeling iron

log

bark

Woodsmen *cut down trees and prepared the wood for other woodworkers to use. This woodsman is using a* **peeling iron** *to peel off a tree's bark.*

shingle

froe

A **shinglemaker** *made shingles for roofs. His workbench was called a* **shaving horse.**

shaving horse

Woodworkers called **wainwrights** built wagons and carriages.

Many woodworkers used **lathes** to carve and shape wood. A lathe was attached to a large wheel. When a woodworker turned the wheel, the wood on the lathe spun around quickly. Another woodworker carved and shaped the wood while it was spinning.

turner

lathe

spindle

great wheel

The turner shaped wood.

Barrels were made by **coopers**.

Cabinetmakers made chairs, tables, drawers, and even coffins!

mallet

spokes

wheel hub

vanity table

A **drawknife** was used for smoothing wood.

The wheelwright made all kinds of wheels. He also repaired damaged wheels.

The blacksmith

The word "blacksmith" is made up of the words "black" and "**smite**." To smite is to hit or pound. Blacksmiths worked with iron, a black metal. They pounded hot iron to make useful objects for farmers, for tradespeople, and for homes.

iron kettle

Blacksmiths made iron kettles, pots, pans, and kitchen tools.

chandelier

lantern

anvil

This blacksmith is working in the smithy.

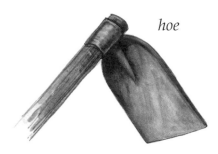

hoe

Farming tools, such as shovels and hoes, were made by blacksmiths.

ball peen hammer

nails

Blacksmiths also made tools, such as hammers and nails, which were used by woodworkers.

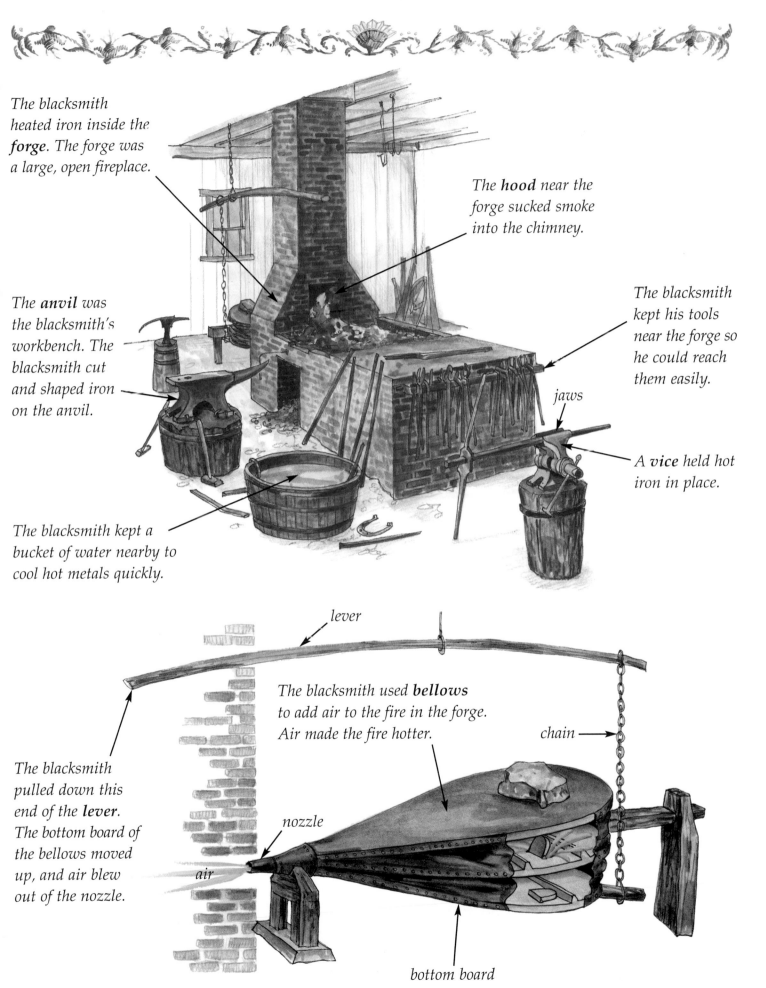

The blacksmith heated iron inside the **forge**. The forge was a large, open fireplace.

The **hood** near the forge sucked smoke into the chimney.

The **anvil** was the blacksmith's workbench. The blacksmith cut and shaped iron on the anvil.

The blacksmith kept his tools near the forge so he could reach them easily.

jaws

A **vice** held hot iron in place.

The blacksmith kept a bucket of water nearby to cool hot metals quickly.

lever

The blacksmith used **bellows** to add air to the fire in the forge. Air made the fire hotter.

chain

The blacksmith pulled down this end of the **lever**. The bottom board of the bellows moved up, and air blew out of the nozzle.

nozzle

air

bottom board

The farrier

tongs

flatter

nails

horseshoes

People traveled mainly by horse in colonial days. Horses needed shoes to protect their feet. The **farrier** was a kind of blacksmith who made horseshoes from iron. He also **shod**, or put shoes onto horses' hoofs. Farriers were very good with animals, so often they were **veterinarians**, too. A veterinarian is a doctor who cares for animals.

farrier

apprentice

Young farriers learned their skills by working as apprentices with skilled farriers or blacksmiths.

Shoeing a horse

1. The farrier lifted the horse's leg and held its hoof steady.

2. Next, he removed the nails from each old shoe and took off the shoe.

tongs

③

3. The farrier clipped the ends of each hoof, just as you clip your fingernails.

hoof ends

③

iron rod

④

4. To make each shoe, the farrier heated a thin iron rod over the fire. He hit each iron rod with a hammer to give it a curved shape.

5. The farrier made a **cat's ear** at the front of each shoe. The cat's ear kept the shoe from slipping off the hoof. The farrier turned down the ends of the shoe to make **heels**.

⑤

⑥

6. He made eight holes in each horseshoe for the nails.

7. The farrier heated the shoes and fitted them to the horse's hoofs. The hot iron did not hurt the horse. The farrier then took off the shoes and hung them up to cool.

⑦

hot iron shoe

8. Next, the farrier nailed the shoes to the hoofs. The nails did not hurt the horse.

⑧

cat's ear

end of nail

heel

Colonial travel

In colonial times, travel was difficult and dangerous. Colonists who lived near rivers, lakes, or oceans traveled by boat. Ships also sailed from Europe to North America. Ships were built by **shipwrights**. On land, people walked or rode horses from one place to another. To travel from town to town, people used wagons or **coaches**.

shipwrights

compass

sails

sailing ships

Stagecoaches were coaches that took people on long land trips. They were called stagecoaches because the distance between each stop was a **stage** of the journey. After a long day of travel, stagecoaches stopped at **inns**, where people could get meals and stay overnight. During these stops, horses were fed and often changed for well-rested horses.

On land, many people traveled on horseback.

hay for horses

stables

water trough

inn

stagecoach

Farm tools

Most colonists grew their own food. People who lived in towns had gardens behind their homes. Other people were farmers full-time. They grew crops for themselves and sold the extra crops to others at markets. There were no machines in those days. People used tools to help them plant and **harvest**, or gather crops. Most of the tools used by farmers were hand tools. Farming was very hard work!

hay wagon

rake

scythe

*A **scythe** was used to cut grain crops such as corn and wheat. It had a long, sharp blade and a wooden handle.*

Ox carts were used to carry heavy loads. The oxen were held together with **yokes**.

yoke

Axes were used to chop down trees and cut them into logs for firewood.

ox cart

A shovel was used to move dirt from one area to another.

plow

A **sickle** was used to cut down hay, corn stalks, and tall grasses.

The **plow** was a farmer's most important tool. Oxen or horses pulled the plow. The plow cut ridges into the soil. Seeds were planted in the ridges.

The blade was called the **plowshare**.

A farmer used a **hoe** to break up the soil and prepare it for planting.

The colonial kitchen

People worked hard, and they looked forward to their meals. The kitchen was the place where people ate and spent most of their time. It was the "heart" of the home. Some homes had only one room, and the kitchen was a big part of it. The center of the kitchen was the fireplace. There were no stoves, so everything was cooked over an open fire. The fire was not allowed to go out because it was difficult to start a new fire.

trencher

Some early colonial families ate their meals from **trenchers***, or bowls carved into tabletops.*

In smaller colonial homes, the beds were in the same room as the kitchen.

People used candles for light. This **lantern** *has a candle inside it.*

Bread was baked at the side of the fireplace in a bread oven.

towels

wash basin

Children slept in the same room as their parents.

The fireplace provided the heat and most of the light in the room.

Jobs such as washing clothes and making butter were also done here.

Most people grew vegetables in gardens behind their homes. Many homes also had chicken coops and dairies. Fresh eggs, milk, and vegetables were used for making meals.

This large home had a separate kitchen house.

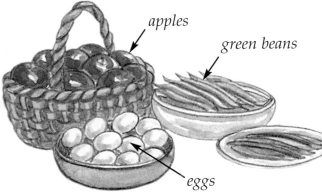

apples

green beans

eggs

spit

A **dog wheel** was used to roast meat over the fire. As the dog ran inside the wheel, the roast turned on the **spit**.

key

clock jack

roast

Bread was toasted over the fire in an iron toaster. The long handle was used to lift the toaster in and out of the fire.

A **potato boiler** was filled with potatoes and put into a pot of boiling water. When the potatoes were cooked, the boiler was lifted out of the pot. The water drained out through the holes.

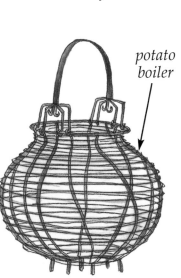

potato boiler

A **clock jack** was another way to roast meat over the fire. The jack was wound up like a clock. The clock jack slowly turned the meat over the flame so it cooked evenly on all sides.

Soups and stews were cooked in heavy iron pots.

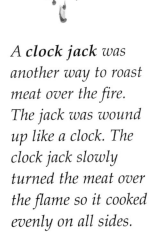

21

Colonial children

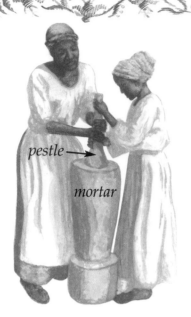

These slaves are using a large wooden mortar and pestle to pound grain into flour for bread.

Most colonial children had to work hard every day. Girls helped their mothers work in the home. Boys often worked in the fields. Some children became apprentices to tradespeople such as blacksmiths or woodworkers. The children of slaves worked as servants in homes or in the fields. Some colonial children did not have to work. They were part of very wealthy families. Some wealthy boys were sent to **boarding schools**, where they lived. Girls did not go to school. They were taught to cook and sew. Some learned to play musical instruments.

Girls helped their mothers prepare the meals for the family. The girl on the left is peeling potatoes to go with the chicken her mother has cooked. The girl on the right is **churning** butter. To churn butter is to pump the stick in the butter churn up and down until the cream inside becomes solid chunks of butter. Churning butter was hard work!

Girls helped keep the house clean. This girl is sweeping the floor.

mortar and pestle

Most children learned job skills by working as apprentices. This boy is learning how to be an apothecary. The apothecary is grinding medicine into powder using a mortar and pestle.

hoops

There were very few toys in colonial days. Children played simple games such as hoops, above, or **quoits**, below. Both games were played using homemade items.

firewood

eggs

pie

These slave children helped their mother, who was a cook. They prepared meals for a wealthy family.

quoits

The milliner

painted fan

The **milliner** sold goods that came from other countries. Milliners knew about the latest styles in women's clothing. Some milliners also made gowns for women, but many just sold items. Milliners sold shoes, fabrics, buttons, thread, and **accessories**. Accessories added the finishing touches to outfits. Accessories included items such as purses and fans. Fans kept women cool and made outfits look fancier.

handbag — *lady's undergarment* — *parasol* — *feathers* — *gown* — *gown* — *fashion doll* — *hatboxes* — *fabrics* — *shoes* — *hat*

Fashion dolls, shown above, were like the **mannequins** we see in stores today. They were dressed in small gowns, which were just like the gowns that women wore in Europe. Fashion dolls showed colonial women the latest styles.

handbag or purse

*A **choker** is a necklace that is tied closely around a woman's neck.*

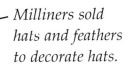

Milliners sold hats and feathers to decorate hats.

Women wore masks outdoors to keep their faces from getting tanned by the sun.

Neckerchiefs covered low necklines.

full-face mask

pudding cap

Milliners also sold children's clothes and special items such as **puddings**. Puddings were soft bumper pads that kept small children from getting hurt when they fell.

pudding

Gloves also kept hands warm.

Women carried **muffs** to keep their hands warm.

Garters were worn to keep stockings from falling down.

stockings

Pockets were not part of dresses. They were tied around the waist under dresses.

Aprons kept dresses clean. Lace aprons made clothing look fancier.

Cloaks were worn outdoors on cool days.

buckle

Fancy shoes such as these were sold by the milliner.

This backless shoe was called a **mule**.

Some shoes had buckles. Some buckles were made of gold.

Women's clothing

pearls

Wealthy colonial women wore beautiful gowns. Most fancy gowns came from Europe. A woman put on many layers of clothing to get dressed, especially in a fancy gown. Women also wore feathers, jewelry, and flowers in their hair. Some wore wigs. Not everyone dressed in fancy clothes, however. Most women wore plain gowns with aprons on top to keep their dresses clean while they worked.

Some wigs were decorated with feathers, flowers, and pearls.

wig

neckerchief

gown

fan

mobcaps

Most women wore **mobcaps**. *Mobcaps were everyday hats.*

A **calash** *was a large hood that protected big hairstyles.*

apron

Girls wore dresses that were like the dresses of their mothers.

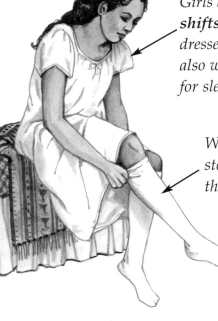

Girls and women wore **shifts** under their dresses. A shift was also worn at night for sleeping.

Women wore stockings on their legs.

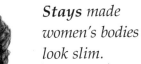

Stays made women's bodies look slim.

Stays were laced tightly at the back.

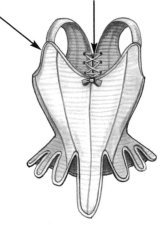

Some women wore huge hats and had fancy hairstyles. Their hair was sprayed gray.

Petticoats were worn over shifts.

a woman's jacket

Pocket hoops made skirts look wider and more fashionable.

choker

Some women wore wigs, but most did not.

Nosegays were flowers worn at the neck.

A **modesty piece** was a ruffle that covered the chest.

What men wore

solitaire

Colonial men's clothing was almost as fancy as women's clothing. Men wore suits with **breeches**. Breeches were short pants that ended at the knees. Men wore stockings on their legs and shoes or boots on their feet. Under their suit coats, men wore vests called **waistcoats**. Most men wore wigs and hats. Those who did not wear their hats carried them in their hands. Around their necks, men wore scarves or ties. The tie on the left is called a **solitaire**.

This riding boot was called a **jackboot**.

This type of riding boot protected a man's knees.

A **tricorne** was a hat with three corners.

cravats

suit coat

waistcoat

breeches

stockings

shoe with buckle

This man is wearing a **cadogan wig**.

A **stock** was a scarf that fastened at the back.

Fancy suits were made from fabrics such as velvet or silk.

Lace cuffs hung down over a man's wrists.

Many men carried **walking sticks**.

bag

A bag wig held the **queue**, or tail, of the wig in a bag.

At home, men took off their wigs and wore cloth hats.

Glasses were called **spectacles**.

Boys wore clothes that were like the clothes their fathers wore.

a man's glove

queue

A **ramillies wig** had a braided queue.

A **snuff box** held tobacco.

a man's **pocket watch**

handkerchief

29

Colonial shops

Colonial **merchants**, or shop owners, advertised the items they sold by putting signs above the doors of their shops. Most signs did not have words. Instead, signs had pictures to advertise different businesses. Many colonists could not read, but they could guess what the signs meant by looking at the pictures. Can you guess which kind of shop or business each sign is advertising? The answers are listed below.

Which sign advertised each of these shops?
1. wigmaker
2. cabinetmaker
3. bootmaker
4. silversmith
5. milliner
6. apothecary
7. inn

Answers:
1-D 5-G
2-A 6-F
3-B 7-E
4-C

*Where would you have
your shoes and boots made?*

*Who made and
styled wigs?*

*Who sold hats, gloves, and
stockings? (See pages 24-25.)*

*Who made and
sold medicine?
(See page 5.)*

*Where could people get
dinner, drinks, and a place
to sleep? (See page 17.)*

Which shop sold items such as candlesticks, shoe buckles,
locks, keys, and bells? These objects could be made of
silver, brass, gold, or copper.

*shoe
buckle*

bell

candlesticks   *lock*   *key*

*Who made and
sold furniture?
(See page 11.)*

Glossary

Note: Many boldfaced words are defined where they appear in the book or are shown by pictures that are labeled

apothecary A person who prepared and sold medicines; the shop in which they were sold

apprentice A person who learned a skill by working for a skilled person for low wages

boarding school A school where children live

carpentry Making things from wood

coach A closed horse-drawn carriage

cooper A skilled barrel maker

gown A long dress worn on special occasions

inn A hotel where travelers slept and ate

lantern A lamp with see-through sides

mannequin A dummy used to show fashions

merchant A store owner who sold things, some of which were made in other countries

milliner A merchant who sold women's accessories, such as hats, gloves, and purses

musician A person who plays a musical instrument to entertain others

servant A person who works in another person's home

silversmith A tradesperson who made or sold items such as candlesticks, locks, and keys made of silver, brass, gold, or copper

slave A person who is the property of another and who is forced to work for free

smithy A blacksmith's workshop

stable A barn where horses are kept

symmetrical Made up of the same or similar parts on two or more sides

tallow Melted animal fat used to make soap

tavern A place that serves alcoholic drinks

tradespeople Skilled workers who made and sold items such as furniture or wheels

wheelwright A person who made and repaired wheels

Index

Printed in the U.S.A.